ON THE ROAD

Fun Travel Games & Activities

George Shea

Illustrated by Jeff Sinclair

 Sterling Publishing Co., Inc.   New York

WE'RE

The _____ family is taking this trip

from _____ to _____.

How Are We Getting There?

We are going by
(circle one)

Our car is a _____
make, model and year

10 9 8 7 6 5 4 3

Revised Edition published in 1998 by Sterling
Publishing Company, Inc.
387 Park Avenue South, New York, N.Y. 10016

Previous edition *On the Road* published in 1992 by
Sterling Publishing Co., Inc.
Text © 1992 by George Shea
Illustrations © 1992 by Jeff Sinclair
Distributed in Canada by Sterling Publishing
% Canadian Manda Group, One Atlantic Avenue,
Suite 105
Toronto, Ontario, Canada M6K 3E7
Distributed in Great Britain and Europe by Cassell PLC
Wellington House, 125 Strand, London WC2R 0BB,
England
Distributed in Australia by Capricorn Link (Australia)
Pty Ltd.
P.O. Box 6651, Baulkham Hills, Business Centre,
NSW 2153, Australia
Printed and bound in China
All rights reserved

Sterling ISBN 0-8069-0316-3

How many people are taking the trip?

1   2   3   4   5   6

The NAMES of the people taking this
trip are:

_____

_____

_____

_____

_____

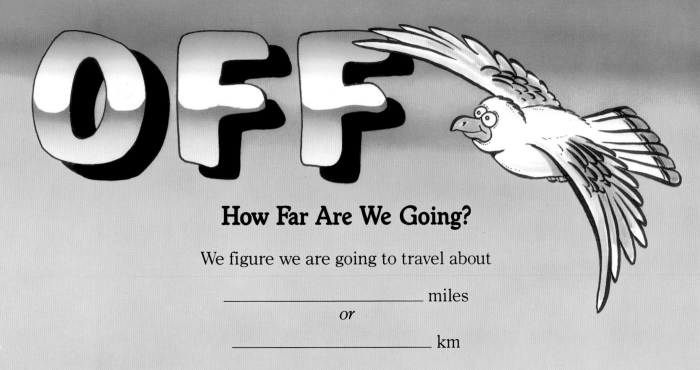

How Far Are We Going?

We figure we are going to travel about

_____ miles

or

_____ km

Where Are We Going to Stay?
(circle one or more)

What Are We Bringing with Us?
(circle all the pictures you feel like)

Anything we left out?

How's the Weather Along the Way?

The weather is   *(circle all the answers that make sense)*:

sunny   warm   rainy   cold   terrible   great

cloudy   snowing   so-so   creepy   terrifying

crumby

How's the Food?

The food is   *(circle any answers you feel like)*:

awful   warm   poisonous   disgusting   stale   great   delicious

creepy   smelly   hard   crumby   awesome   mushy

revolting   hot   weird   unbelievable   slimy   yukky

What Will We Do When We Get There?

(circle any pictures you feel like)

Anything we left out?

What Time Will We Get There?

What time is it now?

It is _____.

We left at _____.

on _____
day of the week

_____ _____ _____
month   day   year

A Contest

GUESS what time we will get there!
Get everyone to guess:

_____ guesses _____.
_____ guesses _____.
_____ guesses _____.
_____ guesses _____.
_____ guesses _____.

The one who comes CLOSEST to the EXACT TIME WINS!

We arrived at _____.

The winner is _____.

Are We Having a Good Time?

So far we are having a
(circle one)

GREAT   VERY GOOD   GOOD   ALL RIGHT

NOT SO HOT   REALLY AWFUL   time.

YE ODD DINER

TONGUE TWISTERS

You stop at a diner that has an odd menu. In fact, it's an odd diner. In order to place your order, you have to say what you want three times quickly. Can you get any lunch?
(Do you want to?)

Crisp crust.

Cheap sheep soup.

Grape cakes.

Brown baked bread.

Clean clams in clean cans.

Greek grapes.

Plain bun, plum bun.

Swiss sweets.

Six crisp snacks.

Three thick things.

You can just say these for fun. Or you can make a game out of saying them. Take turns saying them three times without stopping.
Anyone who slips up on 3 different twisters is out.
The winner is the only one left, after everybody else is out.

FUN WITH WORDS!

Example: Question—How can you write "The people gathered in the square"—using only 3 words?

Answer:

> the
> people
> gathered

1. How can you write "20 miles under the sea"—using only 4 words?

2. How can you write "200 miles above sea level"—using only 4 words?

3. How can you write "30 degrees below zero"—using only 3 words?

4. How can you write "around the corner"—using only 2 words?

5. How can you write "The boy walked around the corner"—using only 3 words?

6. How can you write "She sat on the chair"—using only 2 words?

7. How can you write "The boy sat in the box"—using only 3 words?

8. How can you write, "She drove around in circles"—using only 3 words?

9. How can you write "He was lost in the woods"—using only 5 words?

10. How can you write "She sat beside the lake"—using only 4 words?

Answers on page 45.

You Can't Get to Heaven

One of the best songs to travel with is "You Can't Get to Heaven." That's because everyone in the car can make up new verses for it. You probably know the tune. Here are a few verses we made up to get you started:

Oh, you can't get to heaven
On a crocodile—
Cause the Lord don't like
That snappy style.

Oh, you can't get to heaven
On a hungry mule—
Cause the Lord don't sell
No hungry mule fuel.

Oh, you can't get to heaven
On your hands and knees—
Cause that's the way
You pick up fleas.

Oh, you can't get to heaven
Not doin' what you ought'a—
Cause St. Peter will stop you
Right at the border.

And so on. Try it with the names of cars:

Oh, you can't get to heaven
In a Cadillac—
Cause the Lord will send
You right on back.

Oh, you can't get to heaven
On a subway train—
Cause the gosh darn thing
Is stuck again.

Oh, you can't get to heaven
On a pogo stick—
Cause you'd shake so hard
That you'd get sick.

Oh, you can't get to heaven
On angels' wings—
Cause you and I
Can't grow those things.

Oh, you can't get to heaven
On Santa's sleigh—
Cause Santa's sleigh
Don't go that way.

And food:

Oh, you can't get to heaven
With a pizza pie
Cause a pizza pie
Won't fly that high.

And anything else you can think of.

The Wheels of the Car

This song is ridiculous, but lots of fun to sing. It goes to the tune of
"Here We Go Round the Mulberry Bush." It has lots of verses. Think about
different parts of the car and add your own.

Oh, the wheels on the car
Go round and round,
Round and round,
Round and round,
The wheels on the car
Go round and round,
All through the town.

Oh, the horn on the car
Goes HONK! HONK! HONK!
HONK! HONK! HONK!
HONK! HONK! HONK!
The horn on the car
Goes HONK! HONK! HONK!
All through the town.

You get the idea. You can sing:

Oh, the wiper on the car
Goes SWISH! SWISH! SWISH!, etc.

Oh, the engine on the car
Goes CHUG! CHUG! CHUG!, etc.

Oh, the brakes on the car
Go SQUEAK! SQUEAK! SQUEAK!, etc.

Oh, the radio on the car
Goes BOOM! BOOM! BOOM!, etc.

Oh, the lights on the car
Go BLINK! BLINK! BLINK!, etc.

Oh, the doors on the car
Go SLAM! SLAM! SLAM! etc.

Or do a different kind of verse:

Now the children in the car
Go "NAH! NAH! NAH!" etc.

Now the driver of the car
Says, "CUT IT OUT!" etc.

Or change it:

Now the wheels on the car
Go nowhere at all,
Nowhere at all,
Nowhere at all.
Now the wheels on the car
Go nowhere at all,
All over nowhere.

And the driver gets out
And takes a look,
And takes a look,
And takes a look,
And the driver gets out
And takes a look,
To see what's wrong.

9

CAR ALPHABET...

Can you name a car for every letter of the alphabet?
Example: B __ I C __ = Buick.
The letters Q, U, V, W, X and Z don't start the names of cars. But the names of cars have these letters inside them.

A   A _ _ _ _ R D

B   B _ W

C   C A _ _ L L _ _

D   D _ _ G _

E   E S _ _ R _

F   F _ _ D

G   G _ O

H   H O _ _ A

I   I N _ I _ I _ I

J   J E _ _

K   K _ A

L   L I _ C _ _ N

M   M A _ _ A

N   N I _ _ _ N

O   O L _ _ M O _ _ L E

P   P O _ _ I A _

Q   M E _ _ U R _ G R _ N D
     M _ _ Q _ _ S

R   R O _ _ _ R _ _ _ E

S   S U _ _ _ U

T   T _ _ R _ S

U   H Y U _ _ _

V   C _ _ V _ T T _

W   _ W

X   L _ X _ _

Y   _ _ _ V Y B L _ Z _ _

Z   I S _ Z _

Answers on page 45.

WHAT'S WRONG WITH THIS CAR?!

There are 20 things wrong with this car.
How many of them can you come up with?

1. _____
2. _____
3. _____
4. _____
5. _____
6. _____
7. _____
8. _____
9. _____
10. _____

11. _____
12. _____
13. _____
14. _____
15. _____
16. _____
17. _____
18. _____
19. _____
20. _____

Answers on page 45.

JOKES and

Why did the elephant buy a bigger car?
He needed more trunk space.

Where does Dracula go to get his cars?
To Hearse Rent-a-Car.

What kind of car does Dracula drive?
A Bloodmobile.

What kind of car does the Wolfman drive?
A Furrd.

Why did the silly kid pour tomato juice in his gas tank?
His car had a V8 engine.

Why did the silly kid salute the Cadillac?
He heard it was a General Motors.

Why did the silly kid set his car on fire?
He wanted to fry some wienies on the grill.

What do you get when you cross your car with a Las Vegas employee?
A wheeler-dealer.

PASSENGER: Hey, does this train stop at Grand Central Station?
CONDUCTOR: If it doesn't, there'll be one heck of an accident!

What has a steering wheel and flies?
A garbage truck.

BURT: Have an accident?
HURT: No, thanks. Just had one!

RIDDLES!...

Two fleas left a movie theatre in the rain. One said to the other: "Hey, do you want to walk home or try to catch a dog?"

What's the difference between a red light and a green light?
Boy, I'll never ask you to drive me anywhere!

What is a twip?
A wide on a twain.

What kind of car does Superman drive?
A Superu.

What's the meanest car in the world?
An Attila the Honda.

What's the tallest building in any city you'll travel to?
The library. Because it has the most stories.

What did the Atlantic say to the Pacific?
Nothing. It just waved.

Why was the gasoline pump so embarrassed?
Because it always made a fuel out of itself.

Why did the silly kid go down to the highway with a loaf of bread?
He heard there was a big traffic jam.

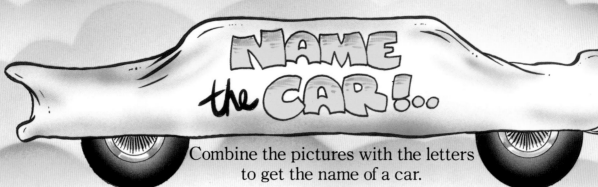

NAME the CAR!...

Combine the pictures with the letters
to get the name of a car.

① = KIA (KEY + AAHH)

②
=
_____

③
=
_____

④ BOOM!
=
_____

⑤ IN OUT
=
_____

⑥
=
_____

⑦
=
_____

⑧
=
_____

⑨
=
_____

⑩
=
_____

14

Answers on page 45.

SIX SMELLY SOX

One person is "It."
The others take turns asking that one person questions like, "What are you going to have for dinner tonight?" to which "It" must reply: "Six smelly socks."

"It" must *always* reply, "Six smelly socks."
If "It" laughs on three turns, "It" is out.
Then someone else is "It."

Who wins this game? The player with the worst sense of humor!

Here are some other questions you can ask "It":

—"What do you keep in your desk drawer?"
—"Who did you spend your time with last summer?"
—"What would you like to get for Christmas?"
—"What does your boyfriend (or girlfriend) smell like?"
—"What do you want more than anything in the world?"
—"What are you going to give your mother for Mother's Day?"
—"What are you going to wear to the party?"
—"What do you smell like after you take a bath?"
—"What does your house smell like?"
—"What's the name of your favorite sports team?"
—"Who would you like to be alone with in the dark?"

Here are some other answers "It" can give in future games.

"Six smelly sneakers."
"Last year's smelly underwear."
"That gross thing under my bed."

Try to think of some funny answers of your own, too.

PICTURE Capitals

The names of some capitals of states and provinces are sounded out by adding the pictures and letters below. You get 5 points for each one you decode—and then another 5 points if you can tell what state or province it is in.

Answers on page 45.

HINKIE PINKIES!

A Hinkie Pinky is a phrase made up of two 2-syllable rhyming words, such as Lucky Ducky.
How do you play? Just define your Hinkie Pinky—or draw it—and the other person must guess what it is.

Example, the definition: An ape with lots of energy   *Answer:* A spunky monkey

 1. A feathered creature who knows everything

 2. Crazy clay

3. A parakeet with indigestion

4. A ballplayer who has been lifting weights

 5. A disloyal reptile

6. Horse in disguise

7. A nasty bottle-dweller

8. A bad-tempered ballplayer

 9. An angry resident of a Louisiana bayou

10. An ancient Egyptian who ate crackers in bed

Try making up your own Hinkie Pinkies. Draw them—or write them or both, and take turns guessing them.

17

Answers on page 45.

WHAT DO YOU SEE?...

ANIMALS	ON THE HIGHWAY	IN TOWN	ANYWHERE AT ALL
(Choose any 3)	*(Choose any 3)*	*(Choose any 3)*	*(Choose any 3)*
black cat	billboard ad for	barber shop	baby
black & white	a movie	bowling alley	baby carriage
cow	blue van	cemetery	ball field
black horse	bus	Chinese	boom box
brown & white	cement truck	restaurant	person on roller
cow	electric car	doughnut shop	blades
brown horse	flashing red	dry cleaners	car wash
crow	garbage truck	hospital	church
dog	mail truck	ice cream shop	golf course
donkey or mule	police car	mailbox	lake or pond
duck	school bus	pizza parlor	mountain
white horse	tow truck	supermarket	statue
	white convertible		used car lot

Each player picks out 3 things from each category—things you might see as you
drive along—12 altogether.
The first player to see any 10 objects out of the 12 wins.

WRITE DOWN YOUR CHOICES BELOW. Keep score by drawing a circle
around each object as you see it.

Player #1	Player #2	Player #3	Player #4

The winner is _____.

Choose one make of car for each player: a Ford, a Honda, a
Chevrolet, a Toyota—or any other makes you prefer.

Then, for 15 minutes—or longer—you get a point every time you
spot your car on the road.

The one who scores the most points wins.

Bonus points: Each player chooses one car from the list below.
Every time you see that car, the player who picked it gets 5 points.
Bonus list: Alfa Romeo • Bentley • Jaguar • Lexus • Mercedes-Benz
• Rolls-Royce

Players	Points	Total

The winner is _____ with _____ points.

FINISH

Answer on page 46.

NaMe the PLACE

Combine the pictures with the letters to get the name of a city or state.

Example: city in Japan
toe + key + 0 = **Tokyo**

① city in Italy

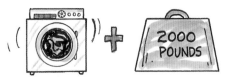

② city in Canada

③ city in the USA

④ city in the USA

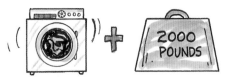

⑤ city in Asia

⑥ city in Australia

⑦ city in California

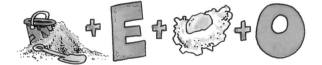

⑧ city in Russia

⑨ a southern state in the USA

⑩ a province in Canada

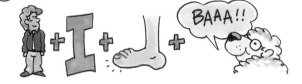

RiGHT and LEFT!

You see a lot of different numbers as you look out your car window.
You see numbers on signs—on houses—on stores and restaurants—on banners
flying above the street—on license plates. In this game, one player writes down the
last digit of every number he or she sees on the right side of the car.
Another player writes down the last digit of every number
on the left-hand side of the car.
Add them up. See who can get to 100 first.
Zero counts for nothing or for 10. Decide before the game starts.

Remember: write down the last digit only.

The winner is _____.

LEFT SIDE   **RIGHT SIDE**

BEEP

BEEP
BEEP
BEEP

BEEP
BEEP

BEEP
BEEP

BEEP

FAM
POU

Who can get to New York first?

Choose your route: Northern— yellow dots
Central— red dots
Southern— orange dots

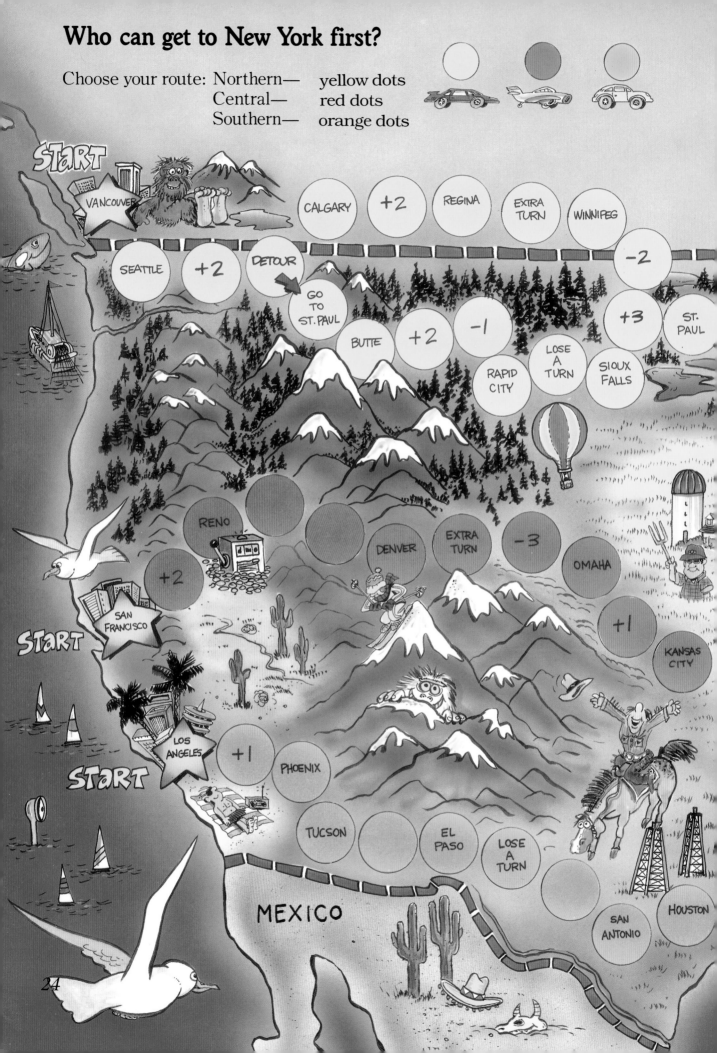

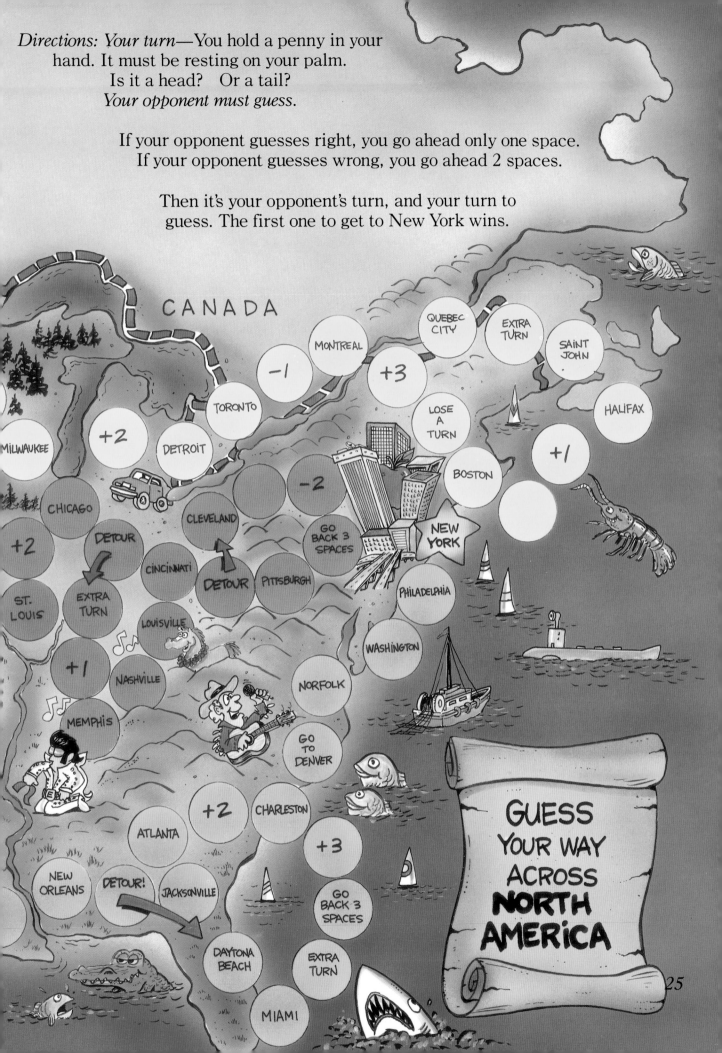

Directions: *Your turn*—You hold a penny in your
hand. It must be resting on your palm.
Is it a head? Or a tail?
Your opponent must guess.

If your opponent guesses right, you go ahead only one space.
If your opponent guesses wrong, you go ahead 2 spaces.

Then it's your opponent's turn, and your turn to
guess. The first one to get to New York wins.

CANADA

MONTREAL
−1
+3
QUEBEC CITY
EXTRA TURN
SAINT JOHN

TORONTO
LOSE A TURN
HALIFAX

MILWAUKEE
+2
DETROIT
−2
BOSTON
+1

CHICAGO
CLEVELAND
GO BACK 3 SPACES
NEW YORK

+2
DETOUR
CINCINNATI
DETOUR
PITTSBURGH
PHILADELPHIA

ST. LOUIS
EXTRA TURN
LOUISVILLE
WASHINGTON

+1
NASHVILLE
NORFOLK

MEMPHIS
GO TO DENVER

+2
CHARLESTON

ATLANTA
+3

NEW ORLEANS
DETOUR!
JACKSONVILLE
GO BACK 3 SPACES

DAYTONA BEACH
EXTRA TURN

MIAMI

GUESS YOUR WAY ACROSS NORTH AMERICA

WHAT'S WRONG WITH THIS MOTEL?!

It's not the Bates Motel—but there are still a few things wrong here. How observant are you? How many peculiar features can you find?

1. _____
2. _____
3. _____
4. _____
5. _____
6. _____
7. _____
8. _____
9. _____
10. _____
11. _____
12. _____
13. _____
14. _____
15. _____
16. _____
17. _____
18. _____
19. _____
20. _____

Answers on page 46.

The LiCENSE PLATE Game

Score points by "collecting" license plates (markers). Here's how:

First see what state or province you are in. The license plates from that state or province don't count.

Next, see which states are the neighboring states. They don't count either. For example, if you are in New York, you can't count license plates from New Jersey, Connecticut, Massachusetts, Pennsylvania or Vermont.

But every other license plate does count. Every other license plate is worth one point.

Bonus: If you're the first to spot a license plate from, say, Wyoming, you "own" that state for the rest of the game. Every license plate anyone sees after that from Wyoming is yours, and you can add it to your score. Of course, the other players know that it's yours, so they are not going to announce that they've seen it. You still have to stay on your toes!

Play the game for as long as you like—15 minutes or 30 minutes—the one with the most points wins. Or just play until someone has 100 points.

Players	License Plates & Points	Total

HINK PINKS

Remember Hinkie Pinkies? Hink Pinks are shorter versions. They are made up of two one-syllable words like "sly fly" or "fat cat."
Here are some Hink Pinks:

 1 A tired old story

---

 2 Fancy dinner for zoo animals

---

 3 A pig in the CIA

---

 4 Where birds go when they get old

---

 5 A noisy vampire group

---

 6 Enthusiastic farm animal

---

 7 A bird that is not bright

---

 8 A street where frogs live

---

 9 Automobile that people go to the movies to see

---

 10 A lamb that thinks about philosophy

28

Answers on page 46.

SPOT THAT CAR

Each player chooses 3 makes of car: one from column A, one from column B and one from column C. And, as in "Spot the Car," you get points every time you see one of the cars. This time, though, the cars are worth different numbers of points:

Cars from Column A are worth 1 point.
Cars from Column B are worth 2 points.
Cars from Column C are worth 5 points.

This game lasts 15 minutes—or as long as you like—or until one of the players scores 100 points. Take your pick.

Column A	Column B	Column C
Chevrolet	Acura	Any pink car
Dodge Viper	Audi Fox	Any purple car
Ford Escort	BMW	Any antique car
Ford Taurus	Buick	Alfa Romeo
Honda	Cadillac	Cabriol
Hyundai	Dodge Shadow	Chrysler Imperial
Mazda	Geo	Corvette
Mitsubishi	Isuzu	Ferrari
Oldsmobile	Jeep	Jaguar
Plymouth	Mercedes-Benz	Lexus
Pontiac	Mercury Cougar	Peugeot
Subaru	Mustang	Porsche
Thunderbird	Nissan	Range Rover
Toyota Corolla	Pontiac Sunfire	Rolls-Royce
any van	Saab	Volvo
	any station wagon	any limousine

The winner is _____ with _____ points.

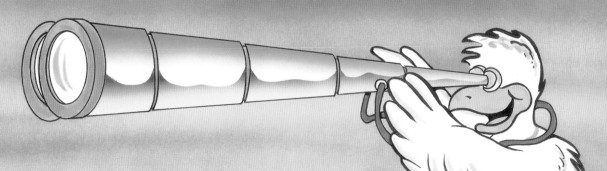

MATCH THE MAKER WITH THE MODEL

Match the model on the right with the maker on the left. Just draw a line from one to another, like this:

Honda — Stealth

Toyota — Civic

Dodge — Celica

There are two sets here of 10 each. How many out of 10 can you get right?

Match #1		Match #2	
Maker	**Model**	**Maker**	**Model**
Cadillac	Town Car	Ford	Accord
Nissan	Miata	Honda	Corvette
Lincoln	Catera	Chrysler	Explorer
Toyota	Integra	Plymouth	Eclipse
Dodge	Altima	Eagle	Cabriol
Jeep	Cutlass	Pontiac	ES 300
Mercury	Intrepid	Lexus	Neon
Acura	Camry	Volkswagen	New Yorker
Oldsmobile	Wrangler	Mitsubishi	Talon
Mazda	Cougar	Chevrolet	Firebird

Answers on page 46.

_____ got _____ right out of 10.   _____ got _____ right out of 10.

ROAD SIGNS

Here are some road signs. Do you know where in the world each one is?
Give yourself 10 points for each correct answer. Give yourself *another*
5 points if you can tell *where* in each state or province or
foreign country you are.

For example, if a road sign is in Pennsylvania, a *more* correct answer might
be: "It is in the western part of the state, somewhere around Pittsburgh."

Hint: All distances on the left side of the page are in miles. All the
distances on the right side of the page are in kilometers.

Answers on page 47.

SANTA CRUZ 78 MONTEREY 111 SAN LUIS OBISPO 243 SANTA BARBARA 349	JOHNSTOWN 74 ROCKPORT 130 BELLEVILLE 259 TORONTO 457
DAYTONA BEACH 93 FORT PIERCE 239 WEST PALM BEACH 304 MIAMI 382	COWRA 311 WAGGA WAGGA 522 ALBURY 653 MELBOURNE 793
WACO 96 AUSTIN 194 SAN ANTONIO 274 LAREDO 426	VAL-D'OR 41 GRAND REMOUS 293 MONT-LAURIER 329 MONTREAL 570
TACOMA 30 SEATTLE 60 EVERETT 85 BURLINGTON 122	CALAIS 40 BOULOGNE-SUR-MER 74 DIEPPE 216 LE HAVRE 320

ODD and EVEN License Plates

This is a good game to play in heavy traffic, especially when many cars are passing you.

Try to find numbers from 1–20 on the license plates you see along the road. Look for them on the *right end* of the license plate only.

One player takes only *even* numbers: 2, 4, 6, 8, 10, 12, 14, 16, 18, 20.

One player takes only *odd* numbers: 1, 3, 5, 7, 9, 11, 13, 15, 17, 19.

Add up your score as you go, or just write the numbers down on the scorecard below.

Playing time: 15 or 20 minutes, or until one player reaches 100 points.

Examples:

Score 7 odds	score 4 evens	score 11 odds or 1 odd	score 12 evens or 2 evens
GS13T67	IT264	SP1511	72P312

You can use each number only *once*, but 2 and 3 and 9 are lucky numbers in this game and can be used *twice*. Why? See the box below.

The Box
Why can 2, 3 and 9 be used twice? To be fair to the Odds.

Add Up	*Add Up*
2	1
4	3
6	5
8	7
10	9
12	11
14	13
16	15
18	17
20	19
110	100
+ 2	+ 3
112	+ 9
	112

PLAYERS	NUMBERS	FINAL SCORE
(evens)		
(odds)		

If you have more than two players, you can form teams.

The winner is _____

odds/evens with _____ points.
(circle one)

Look at these pictures of car parts for one minute. Then close the book. In the space on page 39, write down as many as you can remember. Give yourself one point each.

Answer on page 47.

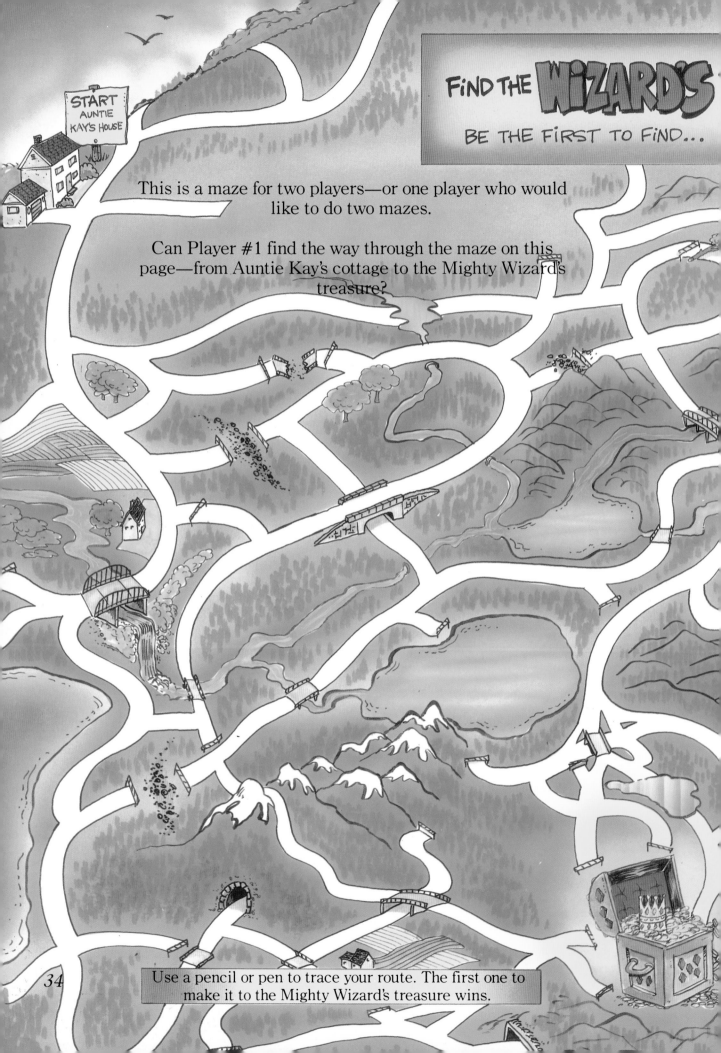

START
AUNTIE KAY'S HOUSE

FIND THE WIZARD'S
BE THE FIRST TO FIND...

This is a maze for two players—or one player who would like to do two mazes.

Can Player #1 find the way through the maze on this page—from Auntie Kay's cottage to the Mighty Wizard's treasure?

Use a pencil or pen to trace your route. The first one to make it to the Mighty Wizard's treasure wins.

TREASURE
THE WIZARD'S TREASURE!

START
UNCLE YUGO'S HOUSE

Can Player #2 find the way through the maze on this page—from Uncle Yugo's cabin to the Mighty Wizard's treasure?

Who can do it first?

The winner is _____.
Answers on page 46.

Car **BASEBALL**

As in real baseball, each player has a turn at bat. Different cars or other vehicles along the road are worth hits or outs.
Here they are:

HITS	OUTS
Red car—single	Blue car
Black car—single	Green car
Station wagon—single	White car
Motorcycle—double	Any truck
Bus—triple	Two-tone car—double play
Jeep—home run	(2 outs)

An inning might go like this:

Jeff is up first. Jeff sees
   a green car—one out.
   A red car—that's a single,
so he has a runner on first.
   A white car now: two out.
   A bus—that's a triple!
One run scores—a runner on third.
   A black car—that's a single.
Another run scores and he has a runner
                on first.
   There's a green car—three out.
Jeff scores two runs.

Linda is up next. Linda sees
   a station wagon—That's a single.
She gets a runner on first.
   Next is a two-color car—that's a
   double play—two outs.
   Now a jeep—that's a home run—
one run scores.
   A white car comes along—that's her
   third out.
Linda scores one run.
   At the end of one inning, the score is:
                Jeff 2   Linda 1.

To keep score for the game, you may want to use this scoreboard:

Players		1	2	3	4	5	6	7	8	9	Total

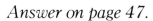

NAME the CAR #2

Some cars have symbols that are easy to spot.

Mercedes-Benz

Can you name the cars that have these symbols?

Answer on page 47.

1. _____

2. _____

3. _____

4. _____

5. _____

6. _____

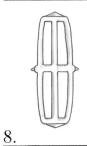

7. _____

8. _____

9. _____

10. _____

11. _____

12. _____

13. _____

14. _____

15. _____

16. _____

17. _____

18. _____

19. _____

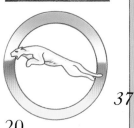

20. _____

37

Who Can Get to 100 First?

Add up the answers to the questions. The first player to get his or her answers to add up to 100 wins!

Example: How many letters in my first name?

George	Jessica	Anthony	June
6	7	7	4

Now Start

Players				
How many letters in my first name?				
How many letters in my middle name?				
How many coins in my pocket?				
How many different colors am I wearing?				
How many teeth do I have?				
total so far:				

Has anybody reached 100 yet? If nobody has, keep going!

How many letters in my best friend's name?				
How old am I?				
How many fillings in my teeth?				
How many different articles of clothing am I wearing?				
How many dolls do I have?				

The HOW MANY GAME

How many footballs,
basketballs, baseballs do
I have?

_____ _____ _____ _____

What are the first 2
numbers in my address?

_____ _____ _____ _____

How many subjects do
I take in school?

_____ _____ _____ _____

What day of the month is
my birthday? (*Example:* 12)

_____ _____ _____ _____

total so far:

_____ _____ _____ _____

*How are you doing—anyone reach 100 yet? If not,
continue . . .*

What grade am I in?

_____ _____ _____ _____

How many buttons do I
have on my clothes?

_____ _____ _____ _____

How many letters in my
last name?

_____ _____ _____ _____

What time do I get up on
a school day?

_____ _____ _____ _____

What time do I go to sleep
on a weeknight?

_____ _____ _____ _____

Now add up your score:

_____ _____ _____ _____

The winner is _____ with 100 points.

1. _____
2. _____
3. _____
4. _____
5. _____
6. _____
7. _____

8. _____
9. _____
10. _____
11. _____
12. _____
13. _____
14. _____

15. _____
16. _____
17. _____
18. _____
19. _____
20. _____

CAPITALS

THE SHAPE OF THINGS!...

Below are the outlines of ten U.S. states and Canadian provinces. Can you name them? Can you name their capitals?
You'll find the names of the 10 capitals in a list of 20 names at the right-hand bottom corner of the page. Write the name of the state or province next to its shape. Write the name of the capital beside the star.
Give yourself 5 points for each state or province and 5 points for each capital.

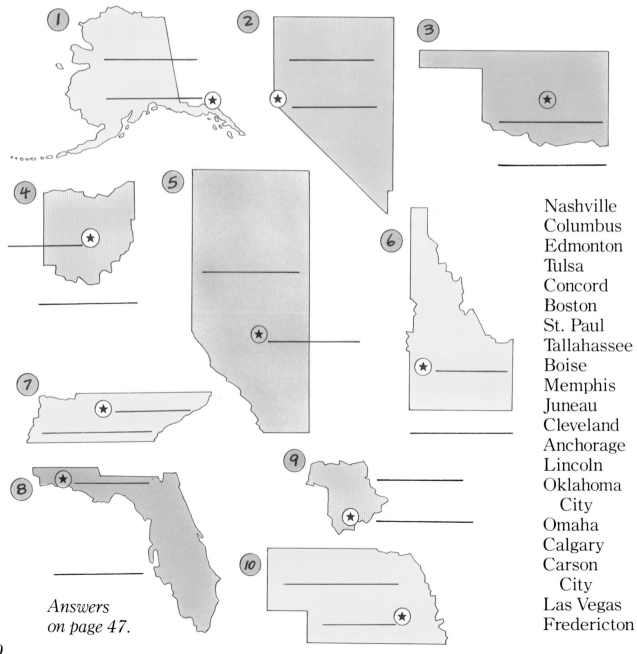

Nashville
Columbus
Edmonton
Tulsa
Concord
Boston
St. Paul
Tallahassee
Boise
Memphis
Juneau
Cleveland
Anchorage
Lincoln
Oklahoma
   City
Omaha
Calgary
Carson
   City
Las Vegas
Fredericton

*Answers
on page 47.*

40

WHERE in the WORLD?

Look at these sections cut out of road maps. Can you tell where in the world you are?

1. This is a famous border between 2 countries. Which state is on the south? Can you name the province on the north?

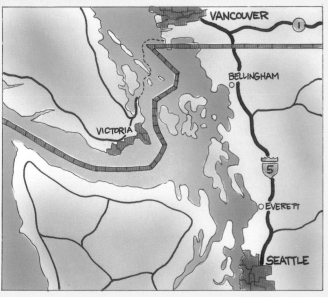

_____
_____
_____
_____

2. Three U.S. states meet here. Can you name them? Hint: "Texarkana" is the name of a small city. It also contains parts of the names of the 3 states.

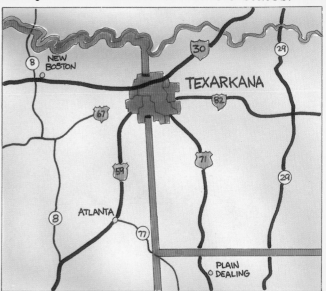

_____
_____
_____
_____

3. Three more U.S. states meet here. One of them is the home of Mount Rushmore. Its initials are "S.D." Can you name the 3 states?

_____
_____

4. Here is another border between 2 countries. Can you name the U.S. state in the top half of the square?

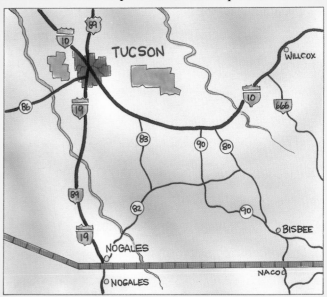

_____
_____

Answers on page 47.

TRAVEL BINGO

YELLOW CAR	A MOTEL	TRAFFIC LIGHT	RED CAR	A CAT
A MAIL BOX	A HORSE	DARK CLOUD	GAS STATION	THE SUN
SUNGLASSES	A BRIDGE	FREE	A CHURCH	A DOG
SPEED SIGN	PHONE BOOTH	BIG AIRPLANE	POLICEMAN	MOVIE THEATER
GREEN CAR	TOLL BOOTH	STATIONWAGON	A HOUSE	FLAGS

These travel bingo cards have objects on them—like traffic lights or clouds that you may see as you drive along. Every time you see one of the objects on your card, mark the box with a big X—or color it in if you have crayons.

The first person to color in or cross out all the squares wins.

Or, if you want a shorter game, you can play until one person crosses out all the boxes in a row—going across or up and down or diagonally.

WOMAN IN HAT	BLUE CAR	RESTAURANT	A BIKE	A NEWSPAPER
A BILL BOARD	A CLOCK	MOBILE HOME	DIGITAL CLOCK	SMALL PLANE
A FENCE	A MUSTACHE	FREE	A HELICOPTER	A BEARD
BLACK CAR	POLICE CAR	BALL FIELD	BIG TRUCK	A STOP SIGN
THE NUMBER 1	A MOTORCYCLE	A CHILD	HITCH HIKER	PICK UP TRUCK

TRAVEL BINGO

TRAVEL BINGO

44

Answers

Car Alphabet

A—Accord	**H**—Honda	**O**—Oldsmobile	**U**—Hyundai
B—BMW	**I**—Infiniti	**P**—Pontiac	**V**—Corvette
C—Cadillac	**J**—Jeep	**Q**—Mercury Grand Marquis	**W**—VW
D—Dodge	**K**—Kia	**R**—Rolls Royce	**X**—Lexus
E—Escort	**L**—Lincoln	**S**—Subaru	**Y**—Chevy Blazer
F—Ford	**M**—Mazda	**T**—Taurus	**Z**—Isuzu
G—Geo	**N**—Nissan		

Fun with Words

1. The Sea / The C
   20 miles or 20 miles

2. 200 miles / 200 miles
   sea level or C level

3. zero
   30 degrees

4. the corner

5. The boy walked

6. She sat

7. The boy sat

8. She drove around

9. THE he was lost WOODS

10. She sat / T H E L A K E

What's Wrong with This Car?

1. Engine on roof
2. Steering wheel on top of the car
3. Side mirror on back of car
4. Front seat facing wrong way
5. Rear view mirror in wrong place
6. 2 door locks
7. Side vent window broken
8. Live cat hood ornament
9. Seat belt around body
10. Antenna on front bumper
11. Tire leaking
12. Door handle is on wrong
13. Speaker on outside of door
14. Car radio on body
15. Leaking oil
16. Tacks under tire
17. Windshield wiper on rear fender of car
18. Hubcaps don't match
19. Tail pipe too long
20. Bird nesting on tail pipe

Name the Car

1. Kia
2. Ford
3. Nissan
4. Thunderbird
5. Infiniti
6. BMW
7. Chrysler
8. Toyota
9. Mitsubishi
10. Chevrolet

Picture Capitals

1. Sacramento, California
2. Carson City, Nevada
3. Yellowknife, Northwest Territories
4. Salt Lake City, Utah
5. Boise, Idaho
6. Hartford, Connecticut
7. Topeka, Kansas
8. Frankfort, Kentucky
9. Lansing, Michigan
10. Salem, Oregon

Hinkie Pinkies

1. Nerdy birdie
2. Nutty putty
3. Burpie chirpie
4. Fitter hitter
5. Gator traitor
6. Phony pony
7. Meanie genie
8. Cranky Yankee
9. Ragin' Cajun
10. Crumby mummy

LAST CHANCE GAS!

A-maze-ing We Will Go

Find the Wizard's Treasure

Name the Place

1. row + M = Rome
2. Ah + tow truck + A = Ottawa
3. Chick + Ah + "Go" on traffic light = Chicago
4. Washing machine + 2000 lbs (ton) = Washington
5. Man singing + A + pitcher pouring = Singapore
6. Can + bear + Ah = Canberra
7. Sand + E + egg + O = San Diego
8. Ma + S + cow = Moscow
9. Ten of hearts + EH + the sea = Tennessee
10. Man + I + toe + sheep going "Baaa" = Manitoba

What Wrong with This Motel?

1. Bear on diving board on roof
2. Car on roof
3. Man reading by table lamp on roof
4. Lettering backward on sign on roof
5. Numbers on clock above door
6. Room number above door has backward number
7. Room number on door is backward and different
8. Doorknob of room too near top of door
9. Sleeper balancing goldfish on nose
10. Picture on wall in room is upside down
11. Porthole in room is open, showing water on other side
12. Light on office door is upside down
13. Lettering is backward on office door
14. Office doorknob is in wrong place
15. Office door hinges are on wrong side of the door
16. Digital clock on office wall shows time 5:83
17. Shark in swimming pool
18. TV set in swimming pool
19. Picture is on TV screen, though the TV isn't plugged in
20. Luggage floating in pool

Hink Pinks

1. Stale tale
2. Beast feast
3. Sty spy
4. Rest nest
5. Fang gang
6. Wow cow
7. Dull gull
8. Toad road
9. Car star
10. Deep sheep

Match the Maker #1

Cadillac/Catera Lincoln/Town Car Dodge/Intrepid Mercury/Cougar Oldsmobile/Cutlass
Nissan/Altima Toyota/Camry Jeep/Wrangler Acura/Integra Mazda/Miata

Match the Maker #2

Ford/Explorer Chrysler/NYer Eagle/Talon Lexus/ES 300 Mitsubishi/Eclipse
Honda/Accord Plymouth/Neon Pontiac/Firebird Volkswagen/Cabrio Chevrolet/Corvette

Answers

Road Signs

1. California (San Francisco)
2. Florida (Jacksonville)
3. Texas (Dallas)
4. Washington state (Olympia)
5. Ontario (on the Ontario-New York border)
6. New South Wales, Australia (Sydney)
7. Quebec (Malartic)
8. France (Normandy)

How Many Can You Remember?

1. Tire
2. Speedometer
3. Gas can
4. Car phone
5. Bucket seat
6. Glove compartment
7. Headlight
8. Clock
9. Gearshift
10. Speaker
11. Ignition key
12. Seat belt
13. Door handle
14. Sparkplug
15. License plate
16. Muffler
17. Steering wheel
18. Taillight
19. Radio
20. Windshield wiper
21. Antenna
22. Visor
23. Engine

Name the Car #2

1. BMW
2. Subaru
3. Volvo
4. Mustang
5. Chrysler/Dodge/Plymouth
6. Honda
7. Rolls-Royce
8. Lincoln
9. Renault
10. Cadillac
11. Geo
12. Lexus
13. Chevrolet
14. Audi
15. Buick
16. Cougar
17. Mitsubishi
18. Volkswagen
19. Thunderbird
20. Jaguar

Capitals: The Shape of Things

(left to right; top to bottom)
1. Alaska: Juneau; 2. Nevada: Carson City; 3. Oklahoma: Oklahoma City; 4. Ohio: Columbus; 5. Alberta: Edmonton; 6. Idaho: Boise; 7. Tennessee: Nashville; 8. Florida: Tallahassee; 9. New Brunswick: Fredericton; 10. Nebraska: Lincoln.

Where in the World?

1. The border between the United States and Canada. The state of Washington is to the south; British Columbia is to the north.
2. Texas, Arkansas, Louisiana.
3. South Dakota, Wyoming, Montana.
4. The border between the United States and Mexico. The state in the top half is Arizona.

Index

Certificate of Travel

This certifies that between _____ ,
day, month and year

the following persons:

_____

_____

_____

_____

_____

_____

_____

travelled by _____ between
car, train, plane, bus, ship

_____ , _____ and _____ , _____ and

completed their trip happily
unhappily   (circle one)
and
unsuccessfully
successfully   (circle one)

_____

U. Gotaway
President,
On the Road Travel Co.